HELENA
Capital Town

**Text and photos by Rick and Susie Graetz
with Tom Palmer and Dennis McCahon**

Photography contributions by
Jodie Canfield, Jon Ebelt/Independent Record, Larry Mayer, John Lambing,
George Ochensky, John Reddy and Donnie Sexton/Travel Montana

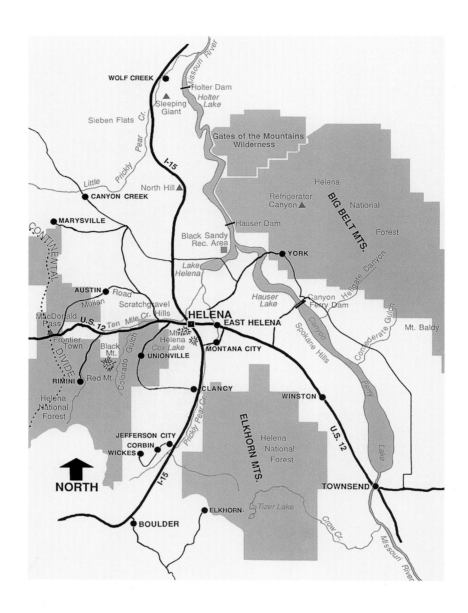

©2004 Northern Rockies Publishing
Rick and Susie Graetz
P.O. Box 1707, Helena, Montana 59624
thisismontana@aol.com

Book design by GingerBee Creative, Helena, Montana

All color and prepress work done in Montana, U.S.A.
Printed in Korea
Softcover: ISBN 1-891152-23-8
Hardcover: ISBN 1-891152-24-6

Front Cover: A view of Helena from Mount Ascension.   RICK AND SUSIE GRAETZ
Back Cover: Laurie, Garrett, Libby and Mike Gurnett try to pick out their house from Mount Helena.   RICK AND SUSIE GRAETZ

HELENA!

This book's initial chapter quickly gets to the point, *"to many people, the capital — Helena — is in the finest setting of any Montana community."*

Indeed, unless they have a political ax to grind, most everyone we encounter on our frequent travels throughout Montana agree that Helena is a *"nice place"* and may be the most desirable town in the state to reside in.

Located mid-way between Glacier and Yellowstone national parks, close to Bob Marshall country — the crown jewel of the nation's wilderness system, within sight of the Gates of the Mountains Wilderness, an hour or so from the stunning Rocky Mountain Front, easy access to several nearby mountain ranges, a short sprint to the Missouri River and several of its lakes, and less than an hour's drive from the slopes of Great Divide Ski Area and the cross-country ski trails of McDonald Pass make Helena a true mountain town and an outdoor mecca. The feeling in the outdoor industry is that more Helenans take part in open-air activities on a per capita basis than any other Montana town.

We have much to brag·about. And with a population of only about 26,000, Helena is the third smallest state capital in the nation behind Montpelier, Vermont and Pierre, South Dakota. We are also well educated ... 30 percent of our population over 25 years old has at least one college degree. Our legislative delegation is considered to be one of the most progressive in Montana. The economy is stable ... 70 percent of our economic base comes from county, state and federal government employ-

⬥ From Mount Helena looking across the Prickly Pear Valley to the Belt Mountains. RICK AND SUSIE GRAETZ

ment and every other year the legislature, 150 strong, shows up for 90 days to pour a considerable sum of currency into the town.

Helena stages one of the best rodeos in these parts with the annual Last Chance Stampede. May witnesses the ever-growing Race For the Cure and a few weeks later, thousands more make the pilgrimage to the Prickly Pear Valley for the Governor's Cup foot races. In February, huskies and their mushers from all points show up in the valley for the Race To The Sky where sled dogs get to show off their stuff.

Our Carroll College is considered one of the best small colleges in the nation and our University of Montana Helena College of Technology receives rave reviews.

We are home to a superior symphony, the Grand Street Theater, Myrna Loy Center, the Archie Bray Foundation and an amazing colony of diverse artists. Athletes, both amateur and semi-professional, find the atmosphere conducive to excellence and give us a great deal of entertainment, excitement and enjoyment.

Then there's the treasured public open space and major efforts to protect it in the face of growth. Helena folks passed a $5,000,000 open space bond issue to give the process legs. The Prickly Pear Land Trust has lent a hand in implementing it. Their mission is to conserve and protect lands close to home including wildlife habitat, open space and agricultural ground through voluntary and co-operative means. They are also responsible for improving and developing trails in and around the town of Helena. Today, with the Land Trust's help, the town of Helena manages almost 2,000 acres of public open space adjacent to thousands of acres of National Forest lands within sight of historic Last Chance Gulch, Helena's downtown.

The Trust is just one example of the many public interest groups located in Helena that go a long way towards creating the very high quality of life Helena can shout about.

We could go on, but let it suffice that this Helena is Montana's best. Read the words that follow and then climb Mt. Helena, look out over the magnificent landscape of the Northern Rocky Mountains and the expansive Prickly Pear Valley that cradles and dwarfs this small community and see if you agree with us.

RICK AND SUSIE GRAETZ
August 17, 2004
Prickly Pear Valley, Montana

THIS IS HELENA
By Rick and Susie Graetz

Beauty shows in all Montana towns. That's just the nature of this piece of the Northern Rockies and Great Plains. But to many, the capital — Helena — is in the finest setting of any Montana community.

The town's location, just off the east slope of the Continental Divide, accommodates a vista for sunsets that can set fire to the sky. One evening a couple years ago, the atmosphere seemed to be preparing itself for a grand spectacle. Out over MacDonald Pass, a red disc began its fading ritual. Overhead, the cloud stuffed sky gave way to a clearing on the west, making room for the setting sun to spread its light. We reckoned it would be worth the effort to climb several hundred feet up Mount Helena's north slope to get the full effect of the promised performance.

As the sun made its exit, bits of orange, yellow, red and purple tinted the western horizon; but the anticipated flame of color didn't spread. Instead, a soft brilliance of gold illuminated the clouds and washed over the town and surrounding mountains and hills. The richness and warmth intensified, filled the air and held. No cameras at hand, the vision etched in our memories, we sat in awe … what a beautiful place, this town called Helena.

On a more recent ascent of Mount Helena, we sat comfortably on a north-extending ridge that falls out just below the cave-pocked limestone cliffs. With note pads in hand, we began a reading of the landscape to tell Helena's story from our lofty perch.

▲ Last Chance Gulch and downtown area from atop the Civic Center.
RICK AND SUSIE GRAETZ

▲ The west edge
of Helena looking
toward the
Scratchgravel
Hills from Mount
Helena.
RICK AND SUSIE GRAETZ

▶ Prickly Pear
cactus, for which
the Prickly Pear
Valley was named.
RICK AND SUSIE GRAETZ

From this vantage point, it's obvious the Prickly Pear is no small valley. Looking toward the northern horizon, it's anywhere from 10 to 15 miles across, and from the west flank of the Spokane Hills, 17 miles are covered before the valley constricts to take Hwy 12 up MacDonald Pass and over the Continental Divide.

On July 19, 1805, Captain William Clark of the Corps of Discovery wrote in his journal, "... *my feet are verry much brused & cut walking over the flint, & constantly stuck full of Prickley pear thorns, I puled out seventeen by the light of the fire tonight.*" From this miserable happening came the name Prickly Pear Valley, sometimes called the Helena Valley.

But long before Lewis and Clark laid eyes on the Helena area, the great Indian Nations, migrating from the west on their way to the bison hunting grounds on the prairie, found a plentiful food supply here. The Blackfeet/Piegan people called the valley Tona, or *"game pocket."*

Our description commences as far to the left as possible where a combination of springs and runoff, above the old mining camp of Rimini, give Ten Mile Creek its start. From this rugged village, it flows out of the mountains arriving at the capital town from the west, skirting Helena's southwest side, then reaches into the middle of the valley. Somewhere near the dilapidated Mountain View School, it connects with Prickly Pear Creek.

Looking out from this ridge on July 14, 1864, one might have noticed four men making their way down Ten Mile Creek (the route of today's Hwy 12) into the valley. Heading up what is now the main street of Helena, the *"Four Georgians,"* as they were mistakenly called, set up camp and immediately began panning the stream gravels for gold. The rest is history — *"Last Chance Gulch and Camp"* was born. In late October, citizens of this rapidly growing settlement, feeling the title *"Last Chance"* was too daunting, wanted a new name. Ideas were bantered, and finally John Summerville came up with the name Heleena in honor of a town in Minnesota. The two Es remained until 1882, when it finally became Helena.

Just north of where the Four Georgians entered the valley are the Scratchgravel Hills — an isolated grouping of rises dressed in a mixture of open parkland and ponderosa pine. Prospectors raked and ploughed the hills' thin layer of gravel to collect gold nuggets. The method was called scratching the gravel and the name stuck to the area.

Hidden in the forests of the Continental Divide are two mountain gaps leading into Helena, MacDonald Pass (Hwy 12) to the far left and Mullen Pass on its right. In 1870, a man named Dundhy built a toll road over MacDonald. His use of log corduroying to cover the muddy spots made travel easier for horse-drawn stagecoaches and therefore, it became the main route to and from the capital. The name came from Alexander MacDonald, who managed the tollgate. Mullen Pass was named for Lt. John Mullen who, in the early 1860s, was in charge of building the military road between Fort Benton and Walla Walla, Washington. The road ascended the pass from somewhere on the north side of the Prickly Pear Valley.

Moving your eyes a bit more to the right, the dark, tree-covered bulk of 8,293-foot high Nevada Mountain comes in to view. This island of dense stands of lodgepole pine straddles the Continental Divide and provides high-quality elk habitat. Black Mountain, at 8,338 feet, is just a couple of miles away and blends in with the designated roadless area of Nevada Mountain.

Progressing north along the horizon, the Great Divide ski area and the heavily mined district and historic town of Marysville — one of the state's leading producers of gold, are partially visible with field glasses. The Drumlummon Mine at Marysville, established by Thomas Cruse, had an output of almost $50 million worth of the precious yellow metal.

Now, looking straight north toward a gap in the hills, North Pass and the North Hills usher Interstate Hwy 15 out of the valley onto the Sieben Flats, through Wolf Creek Canyon then to Great Falls. In 1860, the pass carried the Mullen wagon road into the Prickly Pear Valley, where several years later, other trails, coming from Virginia City and Bozeman, connected to it.

Rising beyond the North Pass, 6,792-foot Beartooth Mountain, also called the Sleeping Giant, is visible. An outlier of the Big Belts, this was land Captain Clark covered by foot while Lewis was on the Missouri River.

According to Lewis and Clark scholar and mapmaker Robert Bergantino, on July 19, 1805, *"Clark probably left the Missouri River near Holter Dam and continued south-southeast to Falls Gulch. He then followed that gulch to Towhead Gulch and down that to Hilger Valley. Clark's camp appears to be south of the summit of the pass on Towhead Gulch about two miles west of Beartooth Mountain."*

On July 19, Lewis's contingent passed through what is now the Gates of the Mountains Recreation Area, which extends between Lower Holter and Upper Holter lakes. It skirts through the northern edge of the Beartooth Game Range and the Gates of the Mountains Wilderness. He was just a few miles east of Clark.

In Lewis's words, *"... this evening we entered much the most remarkable clifts that we have yet seen. these clifts rise from the waters edge on either side perpendicularly to the hight of about 1200 feet ... for the distance of 5¾ miles ... the river appears to have woarn a passage just the width of it's channel or 150 yds. it is deep from side to side ... from the singular appearance of this place I called it the gates of the rocky mountains."*

While Lewis worked his way through the *"Gates,"* Clark, upon leaving Towhead Gulch, followed an old Indian road, which took him from the Sieben Flats area past the Hilger Ranch to the south end of Upper Holter Lake. There, he crossed the hilly lands to the east of North Pass and traversed the east side of Lake Helena where he *"passed a hansome valley watered by a large creek,"* (Ordway Creek to them and now Prickly Pear Creek, which connects Lake Helena to Hauser Lake) resting for the night near today's Lakeside on Hauser Lake.

Leaving the Gates of the Mountains, Lewis took in the scene of today's Prickly Pear Valley. *"... the hills retreated from the river and the valley became wider than we have seen since we entered the mountains."* His journal that night of June 20, 1805, went on to say. *"... in the evening ... we encamped ... near a spring on a high bank the prickly pears are so abundant that we could scarcely find room to lye. just above our camp the river is again closed in by the Mouts. on both sides."* His camp was about one-half mile below the bridge crossing Hauser Lake on Route 280.

Most of the paths and waterways the two Captains followed can be seen from Mount Helena, especially with binoculars.

Continuing the view to the right, the Big Belts dominate the balance of the northern skyline all the way south. Their distance hides the numerous limestone canyons, gulches and lakes among them.

Lake Helena, a Bureau of Reclamation project, is visible, but a succession of Missouri River dam-

▲ The Montana
Race For The
Cure celebrates
the survivors,
memorializes
lost loved ones,
brings hope for
the future and
raises money
to fight breast
cancer.
JON EBELT

◀ Indian Summer
colors.
RICK AND SUSIE GRAETZ

The Gates of the
Mountains Canyon and
the Missouri River.
RICK AND SUSIE GRAETZ

caused lakes — Hauser, Upper Holter and Lower Holter — are hidden. Hauser Dam was completed in 1911 and Lower Holter Dam in 1918. They were named after two Helena mining tycoons and businessmen.

The Big Belt Mountains separate the Helena Valley from the Smith River Valley to the east and the prairie to the north. Within the Belts is one of Montana's smallest protected wild areas, the 28,562-acre Gates of the Mountains Wilderness. If you have a map, you'll be able to pick out two of the more prominent peaks, 7,443-foot Candle Mountain, and the highest summit in the wilderness, 7,980-foot Moors Mountain. In the view field, they are directly above Lake Helena.

Just beyond the wilderness, 7,813-foot Hogback Mountain, shows its long ridge. Visible from the Mount Helena position, the highest summits in the Belts' range, from the closest to the farthest trailing off to the south, are ... Boulder Mountain at 8,819 feet, Mt. Baldy at 9,478 feet and 9,504-foot Mt. Edith. Baldy and Edith are the first to pick up snow in the early fall and the last to loose it in the summer.

As far to the right and south as possible, Prickly Pear Creek begins in the Manley Park area on the north side of Crow and Elkhorn peaks. The creek leaves the Elkhorn Mountains near Jefferson City then runs northward, passing Clancy and Montana City. It splits East Helena before easing through the valley to meet Ten Mile Creek. Together they flow as Prickly Pear Creek, first into Lake Helena, then through the expanded channel of Prickly Pear Creek, joining the Missouri in its form as Hauser Lake.

Lowering your eyes a bit, directly in front you can see the mosaic that makes up the Prickly Pear Valley — patches of agricultural land mixed with a couple of golf courses and a bit of sprawl beyond the town limits.

Two of the most distinctive manmade landmarks, Carroll College, built on Mount Saint Charles, and the St. Helena Cathedral stand out. The incredible church, with its 230-foot-high twin spires, is a lasting legacy from Thomas Cruse. Built as a tribute and a thank you for answered prayers for his success in gold mining, it is one of the town's most visible and cherished buildings. Begun in 1908, the cathedral, patterned after the Votive Cathedral of the Sacred Heart in Vienna, Austria, wasn't completed until 1924. The first funeral held in the new church was that of its benefactor, Thomas Cruise.

At the dawn of the 1900s, Carroll College was the dream of Bishop John Patrick Carroll. The desire became a reality in 1909 when William Howard Taft, the nation's president, helped lay the cornerstone of St. Charles Hall. Because of the school's position on the hill, it was at first called Mount Saint Charles College after St. Charles Borromeo. In 1932, the school became Carroll College in honor of the good Bishop.

To the east, behind the cathedral, is the prominent sandstone capitol building. Construction on the edifice began in 1899 and it was ready for occupancy in 1902. Also located in the capitol complex is the treasure box of Montana's archives and the people's museum — the Montana Historical Society building.

Last Chance Gulch travels upward and west below Mount Helena's east edge and eventually splits into three gulches — Dry Gulch on the south, Oro Fino in the middle, and Grizzly Gulch just behind Mount Helena. Beyond the commercial districts on the east and west sides of Last Chance

▲ Carroll College, one of the nation's outstanding small colleges.
RICK AND SUSIE GRAETZ

◀ The Farmer's Market, a regular Saturday morning summer occurrence, gives folks like Mark O'Keefe and Dave Morey a chance to shop and chat.
RICK AND SUSIE GRAETZ

▲ Spring Meadow
Lake State Park
and Mount
Helena.
RICK AND SUSIE GRAETZ

▶ The Marlows
and Knaffs meet
on the downtown
walking mall.
RICK AND SUSIE GRAETZ

Gulch, the grand, ornate and historic mansions from the town's gold era hold court. Mostly elegant — a few pretentious — their presence is ever indicative of the cosmopolitan lifestyle that once held sway in Helena.

There are two natural *"guardians of the gulch"* — 5,355-foot Mount Ascension on the southeast edge of Helena, and our viewing post, Mount Helena at 5,460 feet on the town's west side. These two summits are part of an unnamed range of mountains that occupy an enormous parcel of ground between Helena, Butte and Deer Lodge. In the gulches below Mounts Ascension and Helena, would-be millionaires dug and scrabbled for gold. Few made much of a living out of it, but they left their heritage behind. The gold in the gulch was the catalyst, but wealth was built from other sources — freighting, banking and a myriad of other commercial ventures. At one time, Helena had 50 millionaires — far more per capita than any other town in America.

This place that grew from a *"last chance"* at finding gold became a bedrock for the state. The newly minted 1864 territorial capital in Bannack was quickly moved to Virginia City in 1865. Helena received the honor in 1875, and when Montana became a state on Nov. 8, 1889, Helena was the temporary capital. But a heated, statewide battle arose between the Butte area *"Copper Kings"* — Marcus Daly who wanted Anaconda to be chosen and William Clark who supported Helena. In October of 1894, in an election, that some say was rigged, Helena won a narrow victory.

From our perspective, the weathered copper domes of the state capitol and the new federal building can be seen. Obviously, Helena's continued growth and prosperity is based on government, both in the form of the state and federal. As of the 2000 census, 25,000 persons called Helena home.

Agriculture also plays role in keeping Helena going. And because the important decisions concerning the physical health and well being of Montana are made here, the town is a mecca for grass roots organizations.

It has been said that many of the state's other big towns have lost their Montana flavor, but not Helena. Growth has been slow and the community still maintains a quiet atmosphere that hasn't changed much with time.

A climb to any altitude on Mount Helena will convince you that this Helena is a place where time and space meld together well.

HELENA — GOLD CAMP
By Tom Palmer

As the story goes, by the summer of 1863, word from Montana had it that Alder Gulch was bearing chunks of gold that could be plucked from the ground by any cotton-picker. Easier pickings than California once offered.

These were radical, turbulent times with the country at war with itself, and the expanding territories also offered a place to run to, a chance to make a life, as opposed to simply living one.

Some seekers organized incredible caravans, and others trekked across the plains alone, leaving their war-torn homeland behind. Many came to find their fortune, many just came.

Every steamboat from St. Louis, Missouri to Fort Benton, Montana was said to be *"weighed to the waterline"* as it pushed up the Missouri River *"with its cargo of human freight and supplies for the mine."* All were bound for Virginia City, a crowded compound thick with thieves, killers and honorable men — but there was no telling one from the other.

Among the throng were John Cowan, John Crabb, D.J. Miller and Reginald *"Bob"* Stanley, typical frontier miners, who would be remembered in Helena as the *"Four Georgians."* Crabb came from Iowa. Miller hailed from Alabama, Stanley from England, and only Cowan, the last of the *"Four Georgians,"* actually came from Georgia.

The four miners were caught, with hundreds of other fortune seekers, in the Virginia City/Alder/Bannack/Grasshopper Creek sluices, with little or nothing to do. Alder and Grasshopper gulches already were claimed and being mined. There were probably as many men in the saloons looking for a claim to jump as there were men working claims in the hills. With gold fever high, the best way to lower the population of the camps and rid the town of idle miners was to get the word out that *"good colors"* — that is *"gold"* — had been found in a remote gulch. Just before the good spring run-off, a rumor was started that some hardluck tramps had struck it rich up Kootenai way, nearly 400 miles north through treacherous mountain country laced with suspicious Indian tribes growing less patient by the day.

It seems that was how the eventual Four Georgians were ushered into the Kootenai stampede.

On their way north following the rumor, the men camped in a valley along the Clark Fork River, where they met a mining party returning from the Kootenai who reported the diggings there to be puny.

That night — it was in May, clear and cold — the word of the failed Kootenai expedition sailed through the Hellgate (Missoula) Valley like the haunting cry of a great horned owl. Realizing they were aced out of Virginia City on a cold rumor, they all must have felt a bit foolish. As other prospectors headed back to Virginia City or other *"secret"* gulches, Cowan, Crabb, Stanley and Miller, probably about June 1, decided together to pan the Blackfoot River drainages.

Without the benefit of trails or compass, and with a waning faith in the ease of gold discovery, the four men followed the Blackfoot River to Nevada Creek and kept heading south and east over uncharted wilderness. Eventually, they reached the Continental Divide, south of the four-year-old Mullan Road. The cold spring rains and low fog made the wilderness trek a physical terror, but when they dropped down the east slope of the Rockies and followed Ten Mile Creek to the Prickly Pear Valley, the elements didn't appear as formidable.

▲ Streetcars ran
from town to the
Broadwater Hotel
and Natatorium
where the elite
stayed and played.
COURTESY MONTANA
HISTORICAL SOCIETY

◄ Early-day
mansions on
Helena's upper
westside.
COURTESY JEAN BAUCUS

Some 19 years later, Stanley recalled the climb down the mountain to the great basin that the powerful Piegan Indians had long considered their *"tona,"* or game pocket. He said the miners' *"gladdened eyes swept the wide expanse of beautiful plains with its threading streams fringed with green-boughed cottonwoods. Bunch grass, fresh and luxuriant, waved everywhere, and herds of antelope, in scores and hundreds, fed unmolested — those nearest turning about and facing the party, wondering what intrusion of man upon their long unmolested preserves meant."*

Time would tell. But as inviting as the valley appeared, after a night's camp and a small bit of panning in the gulch between Mount Ascension and Mount Helena, the prospectors decided to leave and continue north to search the maze of drainages that cut the Dearborn, Sun, Teton and Marias rivers. A more grueling, punishing horseback expedition in the rainy season is hard to imagine.

In Montana Territory in 1864 everything was a gamble and time was the fortune seeker's currency. In this country, you can feel winter coming on even in the sweltering heat of July, and winter and defeat had to be on the their minds when they sat on the bank of the Marias River and decided to head back to the Prickly Pear Valley. If they didn't find gold, they would at least find some solace in its beauty before finally admitting failure. The prospecting was dim, the men desperate and they had begun to call that gulch in the Prickly Pear Valley their *"last chance."*

On the afternoon of July 14, 1864, the four wearily made their way up the gulch where they had camped six weeks earlier. *"It's our last chance,"* one of the men said again.

They made camp farther up the gulch this time and fixed a supper. Some accounts put them on

▲ Historic Reeder's
Alley, a Helena
landmark
RICK AND SUSIE GRAETZ

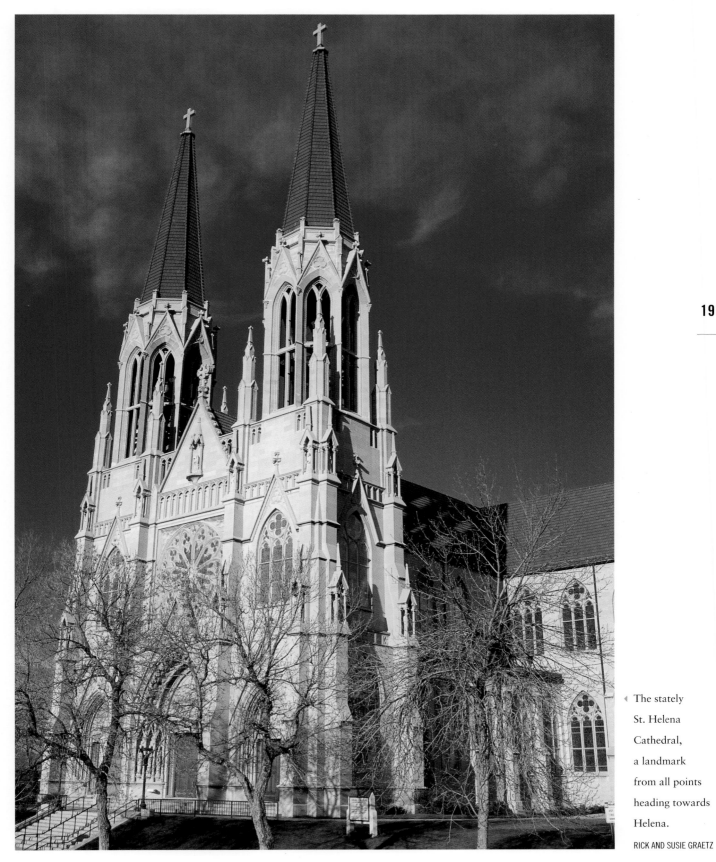

◄ The stately
St. Helena
Cathedral,
a landmark
from all points
heading towards
Helena.
RICK AND SUSIE GRAETZ

▲ The Montana State
Capitol building at
sunset.
RICK AND SUSIE GRAETZ

▶ The Ashley
home in a cozy
neighborhood.
RICK AND SUSIE GRAETZ

the intersection of Sixth and North Park, where the City/County Building sits. Other versions place them at Sixth and Fuller, near the Montana Club.

With the benefit of gracious light from Montana's long Arctic summer days, they moved out that evening to seek the elusive *"colors."*

Stanley, working alone, dug seven feet to bedrock. He panned the gravel in the small trickle of a stream and saw about four flat nuggets. He plucked one from the pan, held it up in the twilight and let it fall back into the pan. It had the sound of good weight and the ring of pure luck.

Calling for his partners, the four dug — near the Colwell Building on today's Last Chance Gulch mall — into the night. Satisfied that there was gold in the gulch they went back to camp. The howl of wolves and coyotes seemed to surround them and after firing rifle volleys into the packs to quiet them, the men agreed the camp would be called *"Last Chance."*

In the following days, these Four Georgians officially laid plans for the camp and the law of the land. Last Chance would be in the Rattle Snake District, which extended *"three miles down, and up to the mouth of the canyon, and across from summit to summit."*

They also set out to define the mining claims that would extend 200 feet up and down the gulch. They called themselves *"The Discovery Party"* and gave themselves first rights to the meager water supply, the best claims and limited future mineral-hunters to two mining claims.

With that official work done and with their provisions running short, Crabb and Cowan — a Yankee and a Confederate — set out for Alder Gulch for supplies and a whipsaw to cut sluice boxes. In a fortnight, they were back in Last Chance, and in Virginia City, the Montana Post mentioned that four Georgian Confederates had struck it rich in a remote gulch to the north.

I have begun to believe that the location of the Last Chance strike, more than the strike itself, made the businessmen of Virginia City tremble. More people were coming to the territory by the day. Last Chance had better access to Fort Benton, Silver City, Gold Creek, Hellgate (Missoula) and Montana City. The geography made it a natural. Smarter and better-financed men were looking for ways for Montana to produce for the States. Gold could facilitate financial backing, but it could not be depended on to make a state's economy — California and Colorado had proved that beyond a doubt. One needed agriculture, skilled laborers, merchants and ease of transportation to keep a western city of the 1860s alive. The Prickly Pear Valley offered it all.

Judge Lyman E. Munson made his way to Helena in 1865 via the Missouri River. He saw the town, built at the mouth of Last Chance Gulch where the Tertiary gravels were bearing gold in nuggets and dust. More than 100 houses were already built and 100 more were under construction. Rent was $200 a month, lodging hard to come by and wages terribly low. Already, speculators were buying and selling claims for small fortunes.

"This was a lively camp," the judge wrote in Pioneer Life in Montana. *"Three thousand people were there, street spaces were blockaded with men and merchandise, ox trains, mule trains and pack trains surrounded the camp, waiting a chance to unload. The saw and hammer were busy in putting up storehouses and in constructing sluice boxes for the washing out gold, which was found in nearly every rod of its valley soil. Men, who had shunned domestic duty over the cradle for years, were rocking a cradle filled with dirty water, watching for appearances of golden sand to open their purse strings to the realities of their adventure.*

"Auctioneers were crying their wares, trade was lively — saloons crowded — hurdy-gurdy dance houses were in full blast — wild mustang horses, never before saddled or bridled, with Mexican riders on their backs, where no man ever sat before, were running, jumping and kicking and bucking to unhorse their riders, much to the amusement of the jeering crowd, and as exciting as a Spanish bull fight."

Bannack, Alder Gulch, Confederate Gulch, Last Chance Gulch, Park Gulch, Oro Fino Gulch, French Bar, Skelly Gulch, Greenhorn Gulch, Dry Gulch, the Scratchgravel Hills, Grizzly Gulch, Unionville, et al., owe their gold and memories to the Boulder Batholith. Their placers all were laced with the gold washed from the batholith's eroded mother lodes.

Helena's bedrock lodes of gold were formed after the batholith assaulted the earth's crust, but before the volcanoes died. Hot springs, fueled by the magma, were fiercely active. Many still dot the region and many geologists believe the batholith is still harboring deep magmatic activity.

Like a pirate's "X" marking the spot of buried treasure, hot springs can pinpoint sources of vein ore deposits. Col. Broadwater's hot springs west of Helena and the Boulder Hot Springs are two of the area's more famous ones, but the entire region is pocked with active and inactive hot springs.

The hot water circulating deep within the earth picks up its freight of elements and minerals being forced from the subterranean pressure cooker. The minerals are transported in solution and carried through a tortuous course of rock. Upon reaching surface-cool rock, the water temperature drops. The cooling water cannot keep the heavy gold in solution, and it is dumped along the course. Mother lodes are fissures in hard crustal rock where the cooling water's mineral freight was dumped.

Water dumps silicon from solution at nearly the same temperature as it dumps gold. Though rare, when silicon is unloaded with gold, it clings to it and weaves its rockmate a quartz cocoon.

Helena miners did love quartz, but they learned to despise it too. Many figured that gold was to be found in every quartz vein. One only had to dig deeper to find the ore. That backward notion tore the heart out of Helena's gold industry in the 1880s. Deep was not the answer. There is no method of finding gold in quartz. None exists. No secrets, just lucky strikes and few of them.

Last Chance, a placer strike, is thought to have produced $170,000 in gold its first year and $10 to $35 million before it played out. Near Corbin, the Alta Mine offered up $32 million between 1883 and 1910. The Whitlatch-Union Mine in Unionville produced $6 million in gold over 40 years. And the Drumlummon Mine in Marysville made Tommy Cruse's fortune.

When the building boom struck Helena in the late 1880s, the Helena newspapers regularly ran short news items on the discovery of gold nuggets during excavation work. In 1917, after a spring deluge, a bank president found *"a gold nugget as big as a marble"* in front of the Placer Hotel. The find prompted *"a placer mining bonanza"* along the curbs, streets and gutters. In 1948, a new elevator shaft for the Placer Hotelwas dug, with only $1.75 in paying dust in every cubic yard of dirt, gold had lost some of its attraction. *"We don't have time to mess with gold,"* was the final word from a hotel official.

During the 1970's urban renewal spree, excavated downtown building sites were successfully sluiced for gold. In the spring of 1985, after a deluge washed tons of eroded soil from the gulches, a friend who lives on Davis Street, on the lower reaches of Dry Gulch, sifted the flood sediments in his basement and found paying quantities of gold dust.

The Helena
Brewers, play
in the pioneer
league.
JON EBELT

An upper
westside mansion,
owned by the
O'Connell family.
RICK AND SUSIE GRAETZ

24

One of Helena's
major events,
held the last week
in July, the Last
Chance Stampede
Rodeo is considered
to be one of the
best in the state.
RICK AND SUSIE GRAETZ

▸ The original
governor's mansion.
DONNY SEXTON/
TRAVEL MONTANA

NAMING HELENA
By Tom Palmer

"The Helena Herald now, for the second or third time, prints the record of the proceeding at a meeting held in Last Chance, which ought to effectively settle the matter."

HELENA HERALD, FEBRUARY 13, 1892

The matter of how Helena received its name was no less effectively settled then than it is now, but it is certain that by the fall of 1864 there were some who showed up in camp itching to sell the first silk hats to dusty-capped prospectors and the name *"Last Chance City"* just wouldn't do. Some accounts insist that Helena was named after a miner's Minnesota sweetheart. Another says it was originally *"St. Helena,"* after the island where Napoleon was exiled. A California man wrote to the Montana Historical Society in 1962 with the notion that the town was named for his grandmother. But the dynamics of early-day Helena suggest a finer calculation. Once it became clear where Last Chance was situated-just a few miles from the Old North Trail used by all of the Northern Plains Indians to reach the buffalo country-those in the Territory with political and entrepreneurial aspirations saw Last Chance as a buried commercial and merchandising treasure waiting to be unearthed. The geography naturally offered north-to-south transit-via the Missouri River and historical east-to-west transit through the Rocky Mountains made somewhat more inviting by the well-known Mullan Road, must have raised some speculative eyebrows. Chances are, an agricultural distribution town would eventually have been established here or near here. But the logical geographic beauty of its location combined with the discovery of gold to hasten and heighten political and commercial development.

By September 1864 there were five cabins in Helena. Bob Stanley and John Cowan built the first two. Other cabins were built by members of a small party, less led than persuaded to the camp by the politically ambitious Captain George J. Wood from Illinois.

The camp wasn't yet eight weeks old, but hundreds of prospectors already had staked empty claims in Last Chance and soon left for better diggings. Still, on October 1, 1864, 200 men were in Last Chance to choose their representatives for the Montana Territorial Legislature.

After the vote, a growing segment of the camp did not relish the idea of wintering in a place called *"Last Chance."* It was simply too crass.

It is a sure bet that would-be merchants and political hopefuls could not live with the deadly ring of *"Last Chance"* when the territory's leading town had a more alluring name in Virginia City. On October 30,1864, a group of at least seven men — some accounts maintain there were as many as 40, but considering the design of the tiny, low-ceilinged cabins, that is unlikely — met in Capt. Wood's cabin. Wood had been stumping for the meeting for some time and made no secret that he was seeking a political position for himself and for his father-in-law.

Also among the men was Cornelius Hedges, a Yale and Harvard graduate who later served Montana as U.S. Attorney, Superintendent of Public Instruction, Probate Judge, Historical Society secretary and a loan association president. Clearly, even at this early date, not everyone in Last Chance was interested in dirtying his hands with placer mining.

The meeting was called to name the town, elect commissioners and authorize the design and layout of the streets. The latter two items on the agenda were handled easily, the naming was another matter. Many accounts indicate that. The gentlemen were discussing the merits of calling the town *"Tomah,"* in honor of an Indian chief who frequented the camp or as a shortened version of "tomahawk." The name under discussion was more likely *"Tonah,"* a phonetic spelling of the Blackfeet word for their Helena area hunting grounds: *"tona,"* which meant game pocket.

Tonah, however, was getting the most reluctant support until John Summerville, described as a tall, angular, frank, intelligent and grizzled Scotsman, rose from his pine block and proposed to call the camp *"HeLEENa."* The men in the room grumbled.

When Summerville spelled the name — h-e-l-e-n-a — the Confederate loyalists could hardly be controlled. The Southerners pronounced the word HELena, as they did in Helena, Arkansas, the location, of a strategic port on the Mississippi River.

"Do you propose this place in honor of that rebel city in Arkansas," T.E. Cooper, the secretary of the meeting, shouted above the rebel yells.

Summerville, whom most everyone called Uncle John because of his years and his friendly manner, did not take kindly to the Confederate association. *"Not by a damned sight, sir,"* the old man boomed. When the room quieted he continued: *"I propose to call it HeLEENa, in honor of HeLEENa in Scott County, Minnesota, the best county in the state and the best state in the Union, by God."*

And HeLEENa she became and stayed until 1882 and the arrival of the Northern Pacific Railroad. At that Point, and no one is quite sure why, the people here began to accent the word on the first syllable and the pronunciation became the softer and more genteel: Helen-a.

In 1906, *"Georgian"* Bob Stanley, who was at that October 30,1864 meeting, Wrote that he *"was surprised to find the accent changed to Helena when it was christened and pronounced Heleena."* It might comfort Stanley to know that town we call Helena will probably always be known as HeLEENa to much of the rest of the nation.

▸ Skiing deep powder
at Helena's Great
Divide Ski Area.
GEORGE OCHENSKI

◄ Mosque-like,
the Civic Center
is home to major
entertainment
events.
RICK AND SUSIE GRAETZ

Helena's Historic Buildings
Writing and artwork by Dennis McCahon

The oldest known photograph of Helena was taken in 1865, when the town was scarcely a year old. It shows a gold camp, a raw and transient place, mostly log cabins and freight wagons. But a close look reveals something more. The narrow street running up the middle is lined with storefronts trying their best to follow the refined architectural styles popular back East. The camp's carpenters had met the demand for such basic items as sluice boxes and flumes, and were now turning out Italianate brackets and Greek-revival pilasters and cornices.

From the start, residents had an eye for detail. They wanted architecture they could enjoy looking at — and since most of them, most of the time, got around town on foot, they wanted to enjoy it up close, at a walking pace. They built to pedestrian scale. They'd keep on doing so for another six decades.

In fact, scale is the one thing that unifies Helena's historic architecture. Those six decades brought us a marvelously unruly bunch of buildings, having nothing in common but the fact that they all invite and reward close scutiny.

The reward might be in the decoration but it's just as likely, or more so, to be in the structural detail. It was assumed that we would want to see how

Sands Brothers Building.

SECURITIES
BUILDING

POWER
BLOCK

MONTANA
CLUB

CATHEDRAL

Eleventh Avenue

Lawrence Street

ATLAS BUILDING

Gulch

Warren Street

Sixth Avenue

Par Avenue

Last Chance

Jackson Street

Cruse Avenue

Ewing Street

Ewing Street

SANDS BROTHERS
BUILDING

HARVARD
BLOCK

Broadway

Ewing Street

MASONIC TEMPLE

BOSTON
BLOCK

PARCHEN
BLOCK

COURTHOUSE

REEDERS ALLEY

EMIL KLUGE HOUSE

BLUESTONE
HOUSE

N

our architecture is put together — and the Securities Building, built as a bank in 1886, is glad to show us. Some strictly decorative work is on that facade, but the main show is about how the stones are cut to fit, how the arches work, and how the parts stack up. All the joints show and different parts are marked off by stone of different texture or color — silvery granite, quarried locally, and red sandstone from Wisconsin.

Uphill to the east is a bigger building made of the same stuff, in the same way, by the same architect, at about the same time. The Lewis and Clark County Courthouse, was also Montana's Capitol building from 1887 to 1902, and lost its clock tower and everything else above the third story to the earthquakes of 1935. Still, it remains a marvel of stonecraft. Take a look at its entrance arches or that little stair tower on the northeast corner.

The Courthouse and the Securities Building are *"Romanesque revival"* buildings. That stony style flourished in Helena in the years around 1890, not only because it was then regarded as the most progressive way to build (and Helena at the peak of its prosperity was nothing if not progressive), but also because so many kinds of good stone were within reach.

Two more kinds show in the 1889 facade of the Sands Brothers' dry goods store. It's built of alternating courses of frosty blue-gray marble, found just south of Helena, and olive-tan sandstone from the vicinity of Great Falls.

Securities Building.

This sandstone, like the red sandstone on the Courthouse and the Securities Building, is well suited to decorative work. All three buildings show us some fine foliate carving, and up where the arches come together on the Sands Brothers' facade are a pair of faces like those once

Main door Courthouse.

30

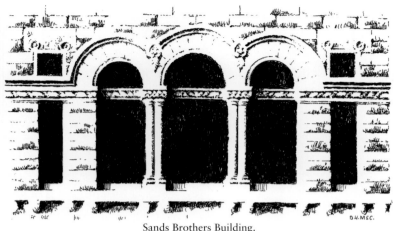
Sands Brothers Building.

drawn on maps to signify hope for fair winds and favorable commerce. The brothers might be recalling the early days of their business, when transport of their merchandise on the Missouri River and overland was as worrisome as any sea passage.

The humble Wolsey siltstone shows up everywhere in the rear and sides of buildings, whose fronts were built of fancier stuff.

Other than that, the stone that shows up in more of Helena's historic buildings than any other is neither sandstone nor marble nor granite, but rather a smoky-red volcanic breccia quarried a mile southeast of town — stuff that clogged the plumbing of a long-gone volcano.

The Power Block, completed in 1890, is built of it. Thomas C. Power himself was part owner of the quarry. He's remembered mostly for his many business successes, but Power also had a keen interest in architecture, especially the Romanesque revival at its most progressive. He brought a firm from Chicago — where the style had begun to address the very modern problem of how to build big without wrecking the scale of the street — to help make his big Helena office block work.

The building's facade is three long arcades, one atop another (an arcade is just a row of arches springing from a row of piers). A tall arcade embraces the middle four stories. It rests on a hefty one-story base, and supports a much lighter one-story arcade on top. The tower at the corner scarcely interrupts the rhythm of those arcades or the sweep of the horizontal lines between them. Instead it bulges streetward just enough to balance the facade's two wings like the spine of an open book.

The Power Block is a big expanse of big rocks, but a graceful one. The rocks get smaller toward the top, and of course they show us how nicely they all fit together, but there's not much extra adornment on the Power Block — except around the entrance arch on the Sixth Avenue side. Here the architects apply an ancient solution to the problem of making a pedestrian-friendly passageway through a thick stone wall.

Working iin the original Romanesque tradition, the builders made high walls that were thick at the bottom to support their weight — but the bottom is where the door had to be. Those builders didn't expect people simply to duck in through

Power Block.

a shadowy tunnel, the masonry mass pressing in around them; so, as demonstrated for us 900 years later by the Power Block, they visually lightened the load.

They beveled the edge, turning the tunnel into a funnel, letting in the sunshine. They turned the inside of the funnel into a set of concentric rings telescoping down to the opening, in effect turning one heavy arch into a nested set of much lighter ones. Then they further lightened the look by covering those nested arches with carving meant to be enjoyed at very close range — leaving no doubt that this was a space to be walked through.

T. C. Power's famous *"block-P"* insignia.

The 19th-century builders couldn't improve on that 12th-century idea, but they could customize the carving. In the design around the Power Block arch you'll see T. C. Power's famous *"block-P"* insignia, the one he'd suspended between the smokestacks on his Missouri River steamboats.

Guests of the Montana Club, across Sixth from the Power Block, walk through a similar 12th-century funnel. The club's splendid Norman-Romanesque entrance arch, built of granite, is really a piece of recycled architecture.

It was part of the original clubhouse on the site, designed by Helena architect John C. Paulsen in 1892. When Paulsen's building burned down in 1903, the arch survived and was simply too good to throw away. The new architect, Cass Gilbert, worked it into the present design, completed in 1905.

Gilbert's design is a sort of lightly applied English Renaissance. Like almost every other architect working in Helena at the time, he took an *"eclectic"* approach to design, meaning that he took architectural history to be a trove of ideas and images, free for the borrowing. That borrowed old-English look is pleasingly clubby; it easily accommodates Paulsen's arch, it gets along well with its neighbors and it fits the scale of the street.

Helena's builders went about their borrowing in many different ways though,and eclecticism itself changed over time. Early eclectics tended to mix their borrowings freely, apply them lightly, add ideas of their own and show off new technologies. That's the sort of free-association that produced most of Helena's historic architecture.

Montana Club

Later though, toward the end of its run, eclecticism often began taking itself more seriously. It took a more focused and scholarly approach to its borrowing, placing new emphasis on finding the *"correct"* historic style for the job at hand and getting the ambience right. If new technology was to be used (as it almost always was) it wasn't supposed to show. That's the sort that produced Helena's most outstanding eclectic building — the Cathedral of Saint Helena, begun in 1908 and completed in 1924.

The cathedral's designer, Albert Von Herbulis, was born in Budapest but trained as an architect in Vienna, just when the Viennese were wrapping up construction of the *"Votivkirche."* A big twin-towered church, descibed now as *"archaeologically correct Gothic revival,"* it was completed in 1879, when Von Herbulis would have been a 19-year old student.

It seems to have made quite an impression on him. The west front of the cathedral he designed for Helena 28 years later looks like a smaller, simpler, tidier and more compact version of the Votivkirche front.

He'd caught the crest of Europe's 19th-century Gothic wave — a complicated movement that was partly a reaction to several centuries of classicism topped by a half-century of industrialization. Builders were yearning and archaeologizing and improvising to get the Gothic up and running again after a break of 600 years. They got it running well enough to cross the Atlantic and to produce, in the hands of those later eclectics, a new crop of cathedrals in some very unlikely places — including the recently wild West. Von Herbulis took it about as far afield as it ever got.

It's usually not as obvious as in the case of the cathedral, but most of old Helena's architectural styles in fact came from Europe. Once here they usually acted like the offspring of immigrant parents, in that they kept what they liked about old-country ways, while otherwise reveling in the freedom of the West and re-inventing themselves.

O.H.McC.

St. Helena Cathedral.

The Romanesque tradition kept its arches and arcades and hefty stone-craft, while growing remarkably flexible and progressive on our side of the pond — and something similar happened to what might be called the the neo-classical tradition. Helena's builders inherited a vast vocabulary of classically derived forms and details and ideas about proportion, then proceeded to have a jolly good time with their inheritance.

That element of fun keeps coming through. Near the Sands Brothers' store stands the 1887 Boston Block, another John C. Paulsen design. You'll know it by those big projecting window structures, called *"oriels,"* on the second story. An oriel's main job is to catch sunshine and light the building's insides, but these do it with panache. They're sculptural. They're exuberant. They give the Boston Block a bold and distinctive profile.

Boston Block window.

Another Paulsen building, the Harvard Block, stands at the intersection of Sixth and Warren. Set at an angle at the corner is another sort of oriel, built of brick and sandstone and held up by fanciful iron uprights. It once had a cupola on top, shaped like a cowbell. It's one of old Helena's street-corner towers.

Street corners were magnets when people got around town on foot and when communication was mostly a matter of face-to-face meeting. They were centers of urban life. Builders liked to put doorways there, on the bevel, facing toward the middle of the intersection, then further mark the spot with some sort of architectural assertion overhead, often a projecting tower-like structure.

Variations on that theme show also on the Power Block and the Securities Building. Standing side-by-side on Broadway between Jackson and Cruse are two more buildings that look like they're having a good time — the 1885 Masonic Temple on the left and the 1887 Parchen Block on the right. They offer an entertaining mix of structural and decorative detail, upstairs and down.

Harvard Block window.

Parchen Block arch and pillar.

Downstairs is a confident display of 1880s storefront technology — open iron frames filled with glass, to let in lots of light — and upstairs are cheery compositions made up of all sorts of classically derived forms, plus a touch of the Romanesque. Formal consistency of style doesn't really matter here. These are eclectic facades of the earlier sort. What matters is that they stack up handsomely and are fun to look at.

That's what matters also at the 1888 Atlas Block, nearby on the Gulch. This time the facade's detail is mostly Romanesque. That beautiful round arch downstairs — 39 wedges of Tenmile granite spanning 18 feet — seems to have been put there just to show us what a fine thing an arch can be.

Upstairs is a demonstration of the ancient idea that a building's outside should tell a story having something to do with what goes on inside. In this case it's a story of fire insurance.

The figure carved at the center of the third story is Atlas himself. On his back he supports a column topped, on the cornice, with an urn that symbolizes the world. A salamander, ancient symbol of fire, is trying to slither down into the urn, but he's held off by a pair of winged dragons (one has lost its wings) that represent the protection provided by fire insurance, sold by one S. J. Jones whose office was in the building.

The Atlas Block was probably designed by James Stranahan, a free-thinking Helena architect known otherwise for a pair of buildings that stray even further from the conventions of formal style — the Bluestone House, high on the side of Firetower Hill, and the Diamond Block, on Sixth Avenue

Atlas Building.

near the Montana Club.

The 1890 Bluestone House is left plain on purpose, to show off its honest workmanship and the beauty of its cool blue limestone, which was quarried just a few hundred yards away at the bottom of the gulch. It's stuff that doesn't lend itself to fancier treatment.

The 1889 Diamond Block makes another show of local stone — this time more of that red volcanic breccia from T. C. Power's quarry — but it also gives us a set of extraordinary two-story oriels. These are lightly built affairs, clad in tooled copper, that appear to spring from recesses in the rugged stone wall. The name *"Diamond Block"* might refer to the tiny beveled mirrors set in the face of each one, or maybe to the glassy oriels themselves — all those facets to catch the light.

The gulch-bottom quarry that produced Stranahan's blue limestone belonged to a Prussian immigrant named Emil Kluge, who also made a more personal contribution to the town's architecture. His own house, just south of the quarry, started out as a second-hand log cabin, but when Kluge added an upper story, around 1890, he built a sturdy frame of timbers and then filled the spaces between them with brick. It's a piece of genuine *"half timber"* construction, an old technique widespread in Europe but uncommon on our side of the Atlantic, and rare indeed in the Montana Rockies.

Atlas Building detail.

Diamond Block windows.
Below: Emil Kluge House.

Clockwise from top left: Bluestone House window; Bluestone House; and Atlas Block detail.

Another builder who started with a second-hand log cabin was Louis Reeder, an eminently frugal bachelor from Bucks County, Pennsylvania. You can still see the cabin that served as the nucleus for what's now known as *"Reeder's Alley."* It's wedged between a pair of his brick-and-stone buildings high on the Alley's upper level.

D.H.M&C.   Reeder's Alley.

Reeder's Alley is pedestrian scale at its plainest. Apparently it never occurred to Reeder that anyone would visit the place except on foot, so he was free to strike an amiable compromise with topography. He let bedrock set the rules. He abandoned every standard notion of what a street ought to be, letting it pinch down to a slot only a few feet wide, or dissolve altogether into a stairway scaling an outcrop.

In return, the site's bedrock served as his building material. Reeder's gully runs along the contact between two different kinds of stone — Flathead Quartzite on the north and Wolsey siltstone on the south — so he built with the quartzite along the north bank, and with the siltstone, plus odd lots of brick, along the south bank.

The only way to see Reeder's work is to go there on foot — and that's also the best way to see the rest of Helena's historic architecture. It's made to be seen that way. It holds its rewards for those who'll take a close look, at a walking pace.

D.H.M&C.

Reeder's Alley.

Mount Helena and The Ridge Line Trail
by Rick and Susie Graetz

"Do not deny yourself the healthy pleasure of the. .. delightful walk. Go all and go often." This invitation to climb Mount Helena was extended to the people of Helena almost 100 years ago.

Today recreationists of all ages are using the mountain in increasing numbers. The original trail that passes the limestone caves on its way to the summit and an extension of it along the ridge line heading south out of Helena, is now called the Mount Helena National Recreation Trail.

Almost immediately after the discovery of gold in Last Chance Gulch in 1864, Mount Helena became an important part of the town that grew from the find. Its trees were cut for mine timbers and cabins and its limestone used for building and mining purposes.

The mountain also played a part in celebrations and revelry. In 1875, the Helena Daily Herald had a piece on a *"Genuine Frolic."* They were describing a hike to the summit by fifteen to twenty *"ladies and gentlemen"* for a picnic. Some hiked, some rode horses. The paper said that *"any young lady who can ascend and descend Mount Helena without a murmur is capable of accomplishing almost any feat of pedestrianism."* It went on to say, *"a lunch capable of satiating the keen appetites that were engendered by ascending this precipicious mount"* was served long with two kegs of Kessler's 3X Lager Beer and a dozen bottles of Heidsick's. When *"night had drawn her sable curtain down there were bonfires and luminations, and a brilliant display of pyrotechnics, which were generally observed in Helena and greatly admired."*

In 1883, members of a bicycle club tested the mountain, but most of the folks who used the peak did so because of the great views and peace a trip to the top brought.

In the September 1st, 1882 Helena Daily Herald readers were encouraged to indulge themselves in an hour's walk to the top of Mount Helena where they could *"witness a revelation of greater beauty than can be found in all the art galleries on both continents,"* and see the first signs of the railroad, bringing with it the promise of *"deliverance, power, wealth and prosperity."* In 1882 and 1883, the Northern Pacific Railway was making its way across the Helena valley. Many Helena residents climbed the mountain to watch its progress.

Although it's possible that the natives used Mount Helena before white men entered the valley, no evidence has been found. In 1949, Dr. Carling Malouf searched the cave at the *"Devil's Kitchen"* area for evidence. Even though he dug a pit of more than ten feet deep he only uncovered animal bones.

In an article written for the Helena Independent about 25 years after the founding of Helena, a man who had traveled through the area a year before the discovery of gold wrote about their hunting party being attacked by Indians. He said they escaped from the Indians and took refuge in a cave on Mount Helena. They had been there before and knew of a food cache.

Perhaps the most significant celebration on the mountain was on the evening of November 12, 1894. Helena had just won out over Anaconda to be named the capital of Montana. That night an enormous bonfire was set off on the summit to announce the victory.

In the first year of Helena's existence, the primary use of water was to wash gold from the gravel of the Gulch, causing a shortage of drinking water. To partially solve the problem, the Yaw Yaw ditch

▲ The last light of
day illuminates
the upper
reaches of
Mount Helena.
RICK AND SUSIE GRAETZ

◄ Kayakers on
Spring Meadow
State Park on
Helena's west
edge.
RICK AND SUSIE GRAETZ

was established flowing out of Ten Mile creek from the west and along the base of Mount Helena, the approximate site of the current Le Grande Cannon Road.

Photos taken in the 1870s show an almost bald massif. Wood cutting wasn't the only cause of the denuding of the mountain. Many fires occurred, including a rash of them between 1898 and 1901. These fires finished off trees the woodcutters didn't get to. The ensuing grassy slopes attracted cattle, sheep, horses and goats. The largest recorded fire on Mount Helena began on August 4 in 1900 when small boys playing with matches set fire to dry grasses. This fire was the catalyst to get the leadership of Helena to act on a plan to replant the trees and turn the mountain into a public park. In 1905 the Helena City Council adopted a resolution authorizing the mayor to file a claim for 160 acres in the park under an *"Act to authorize entry of the public lands by incorporated cities and towns for cemetery and park purposes."*

The citizens of Last Chance Gulch had great pride in their mountain and elaborate plans were made to enhance the place. A headline appeared in the January 27, 1890 issue of the Daily Independent ... *"A Gravity Railroad — Proposition looking to the establishment of a great pleasure resort on Mount Helena ... A Railway to be built to carry passengers to the top every ten minutes ... Beautiful gardens and an astronomical observatory — grandeur of the surrounding country."* The article went on to say *"It is proposed to make Mount Helena a pleasure resort second to none in the country. The main feature will be a series of pleasure gardens and a fine astronomical observatory where people can spend hours in delightful recreation; an elegant hotel and all other adjuncts that are deemed necessary.*

"The projected gravity railway belongs to a class of which very few examples exist, but which are destined to become more and more common, whose purpose is to merely carry pleasure travel and do it without the more or less disagreeable adjuncts which are inseparable from the use of a locomotive." Eventually this plan and others that would have developed the mountain were scrapped in favor of creating a natural mountain park.

The owner of the Helena Independent, John S. Neill, is generally credited with the idea to form a park on the mountain. The Helena Improvement Society, led by Harvey L. Glenn began the planning. While efforts were underway, it was discovered that there was actual ownership of land on the mountain. The Society began soliciting a donation of the land for the park and received permission to proceed. A Summit House was planned and designed by J. H. Kent, one of the state Capitol Building architects. In August of 1903, work began to establish a trail to the summit. The successful bidder did the job for $300 in one month's time. The original trail, that flows on the north side of the mountain, just below the limestone caves, still exists; and it is misnamed the 1906 Trail.

The park and the Summit Pavilion were dedicated on July 4, 1904. Almost 200 residents climbed to the top for the ceremony. It was said that the event was postponed for 30 minutes *"in deference to pedestrians who could be seen, still making their way up the mountain."* Less than two weeks after the dedication of the Shelter House, lightning struck it, leaving it *"slightly twisted and out of shape."* Rough weather on the summit and vandals continued to destroy what was left. By the 1930s it had disappeared.

With their park completed, the citizens and especially the Helena Improvement Society turned their mind set to the treeless slopes and brought the problem to the attention of the newly created Forest Service. In 1905, the Improvement Society wrote to the legendary Chief Forester Gifford Pinchot to

▲ Arrowleaf
balsamroot
blooms in
profusion on
Mount Helena's
slopes in the
spring.
RICK AND SUSIE GRAETZ

◄ Tara Clark picks
a bouquet on
Mount Helena's
lower slopes.
RICK AND SUSIE GRAETZ

44

▲ Looking south
from the summit
of Mount
Helena
RICK AND SUSIE GRAETZ

▶ Looking North
toward the Big
Belt Mountains
from the Mount
Helena Ridgeline
Trail.
RICK AND SUSIE GRAETZ

"elicit the most hardy expressions of the departments desire to demonstrate upon Mount Helena the astonishing results achieved by the expert foresters of the Department of the Interior." The Forest Service responded and in June of 1905 a forester was sent to Helena to begin planning for a replanting. In 1906, 10,000 Ponderosa pine and 20,000 Douglas-fir seedlings were planted. Workers were paid $2.50 per day for the two-day job.

Actually, the first efforts to replant Mount Helena took place on Arbor Day in 1899. Helena school children headed up the gulch that faced the town, each with a basket holding evergreen seedlings. To mark the occasion, and to accompany the working children, Fred Kuphal, who went on to national fame, serenaded them with music from his classic violin. Many of these trees are still surviving today and are known as the Fred Kuphal Grove.

The white H on one of the east facing slopes has been a prominent part of the Mountain since 1924. The rock structure is a high school tradition and its annual painting honors the current graduating class. In recent years, the practice has been on the decline, however.

The precipitous terrain of the mountain has challenged walkers, bikers and runners since Helena's inception. The first Mount Helena Race, was held on April 9, 1916. A *"west coast pro"* made two training runs to the top of the mountain. He was expected to win, however on race day, Ben Burgess, a Helena boy captured the meet in *"handy fashion"* in a time of 30 minutes 58 seconds. The visiting runner came in third with a time of 36 minutes 34 seconds. It's not known how many years the event took place, but for quite a while it was absent from Helena until it's 1975 revival. Bill Lannan, won that race.

The historic Mount Helena Trail made its way into the National Recreational Scenic Trail System on March 16, 1979 in an order signed by Secretary of the Interior Cecil Andrus. The designation was not only for the original Mount Helena route but also for its extension that heads on the ridge in a southwesterly direction for six miles above Grizzly Gulch. The Trail was formally dedicated on Friday, June 8, 1979.

THE MOUNT HELENA TRAILS

Primary access to the mountain is from the Adams Street Parking Area, reached through the Reeder's subdivision. Just beyond the old Federal Building on Park, a road turns right, through the development, to the Mount Helena Park entrance. This trailhead features a kiosk displaying a map of the mountain and historic information. The mountain's main trail system leads out from here. Another entry way is through the subdivision just above the Le Grande Cannon Road Junction with Henderson. The trail from here goes through the open hills on the mountains west side. In the winter this segment can offer good skiing, especially after a new snow fall.

The Adams Street and Le Grande Cannon trailheads both sit at about 4,300 feet and the gain to the 5,468-foot summit is 1,088 feet. The 1906 Trail, reached from the Adams Street point, has the easiest grade. To fully appreciate your town park explore all of the routes. There are ten official trails, and each has its own perspective on the area.

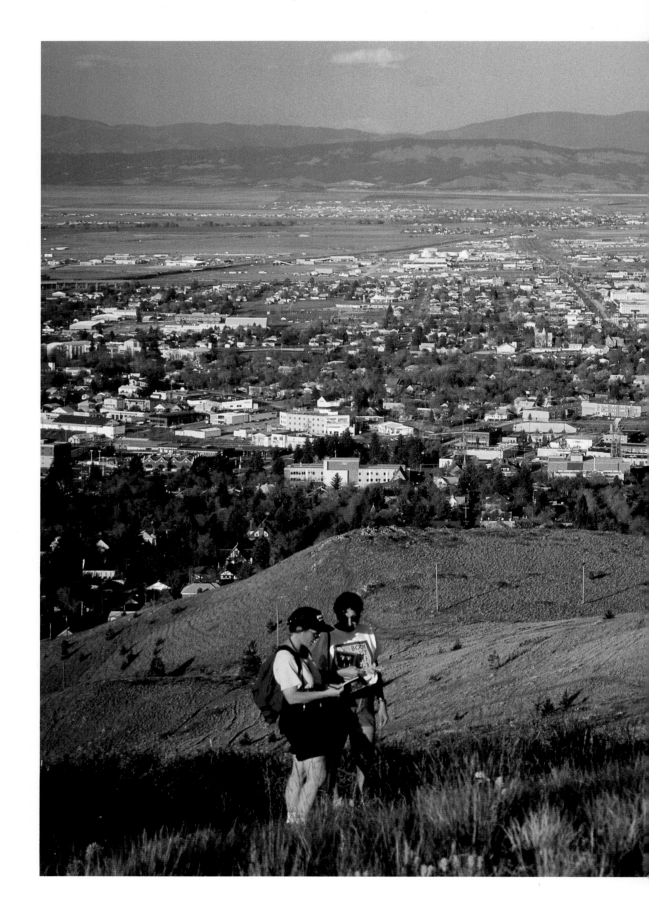

▶ Hiking the trails
of Mount Helena
is a favorite pastime
in any season.
RICK AND SUSIE GRAETZ

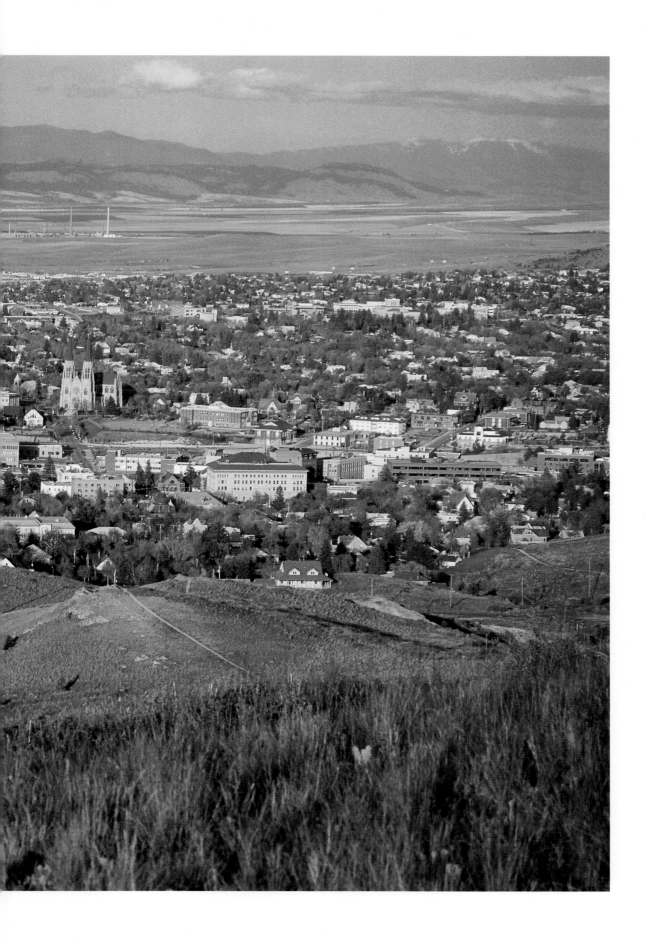

▶ Taking the easy
way down
Mount Helena
– Missie Clark
hitches a ride
from her proud
grandfather.
RICK AND SUSIE GRAETZ

THE RIDGE TRAIL

The trails on Mount Helena itself are by far the most popular and it's a rare morning or evening when you don't encounter fellow hikers. The much lesser used southwesterly extension of the Mount Helena National Recreation Trail branches out for an additional six miles beyond the mountain. Many of us who see it refer to the route as *"The Ridge Trail,"* as for most of its journey it follows a divide or ridge line from above Park City to Mount Helena's west side.

Some of the best views of the Helena area and the surrounding mountains and forests can be observed for most of the way. Enroute you will find evidence of Helena's early mining days, encountering discovery pits and remnants of small shafts. And like the Mount Helena trails, the great display of wildflowers in spring and early summer add wonderful color to your hike.

It is advisable to start out on this path from the Grizzly Gulch end, as after you attain the ridge, it is mostly a downhill grade back towards town. To reach the trailhead from a starting point at the corner of Wong and Park, by the library, head up the Gulch toward Unionville, baring right where the road splits. The road on the right is Grizzly Gulch. It is 4.8 miles from the library to a group of mailboxes on the Grizzly Gulch Road. Turn right at the boxes, staying on the main road for .5 miles and then turn right at the trail sign into a parking area. The track goes left up the hill a short way and then makes a sharp right following gentle switchbacks to the top. Up on the top and just beyond the trail, are several promontories giving you some great views looking back into the mountains to the south of town.

▲ The Whittenberg family on the Ridgeline Trail south of Mount Helena.

RICK AND SUSIE GRAETZ

▲ Bitterroot,
Montana's state
flower, grows
profusely on
Mount Helena
and other areas
around town.
RICK AND SUSIE GRAETZ

▶ Kara Graetz
takes a break on
the trail up Mount
Helena.
RICK AND SUSIE GRAETZ

This route is immensely enjoyable and is open country for a good portion of its way. Anyone who can walk a few miles can handle it. Take plenty of water, snacks, a camera, binoculars and your time. Allow up to four hours to complete the seven-mile journey. Shuttling cars by leaving one in the Adams Street Parking Area works best.

You need not climb Mount Helena to reach the trail's end as the ridge route connects into all the other trails on the mountain. Take the first main path to the left once you reach the mountain's westside saddle. It will lead you down the switchbacks on the Prairie Trail to the parking lot terminus.

Dennis McCahon, in his newspaper The Occasional Magpie, published a great deal of information on Mount Helena's rocks and trees. Borrowing from what he has compiled, the following describes a few interesting facts about your park, your mountain and your Ridge Trail.

Mount Helena's rocks stand out by way of the towering cliffs on the north face and those on the peak. The mountain consists of seven formations of sedimentary rocks, mostly in the form of very old limestone. The prominent cliffs are made of Meagher Limestone. This formation is over 600 feet thick, but only the upper several hundred are exposed.

Wolsey rock, not as noticeable on the mountain as the Meagher, but evident, played a major role in the building of old Helena. This beautiful stone with its mixed shades of gray, ocher and green can be seen in several buildings including the side walls of the Iron Front building and inside the Windbag. It weathers to a very rich brown color. The Wolsey was quarried in the area of the Adams Street Parking Area and the Reeder's subdivision.

Blue-gray Hasmark Dolomite crowns the summit and is exposed along the Hogback trail. This stone was cooked, for the lime used in mortar, in the kilns found in Grizzly Gulch.

Almost all the trees on Mount Helena and along the lower reaches of the Ridge Trail are either Ponderosa pine or Douglas-fir. Ponderosa pine dominates the majority of the slopes. Douglas-fir inhabits the north facing areas. Most of Mount Helena's trees are relatively new. However, the Douglas-firs growing in the area of the cliffs and just to the west of there may have been around in 1864. They are the tallest grove of trees on the mountain. The largest single tree, a Ponderosa pine, is found just below the junction of the Prairie and Quartzite trails.

The trees, the rocks, the spring and summer flowers, views of mountains carpeted in trees and the expanse of the Prickly Pear Valley add up to make the Mount Helena trail system a very special place. We can't think of any other town in the U.S. that has such a magnificent mountain designated as a town park. Any Helenan with the ability to walk, young or old, owes it to themselves to explore their ridge line and mountain. And in doing so you'll meet many of Helena's fun people who make walking on this mountain an almost daily affair, no matter what the weather or time of the year.

The authors would like to thank Dennis McCahon for all of his information both historical and current day and George Schunk for his data on the National Recreation Trail.

THE BIG BELT MOUNTAINS
by Rick and Susie Graetz

Looking out from the rise of the town of Helena, across the Prickly Pear Valley, the northeast and eastern horizon is dominated by most of the 80-mile length of the Big Belt Mountains. Survey this skyline from the top of Mount Helena and you'll see the entire massif.

Helena, East Helena and Townsend folks claim this uplift as their own and easily recognize its many distinct high points. Whether peacefully resting on his lofty bed of green, shaking the valley with his thunderous snores or cuddled under a coverlet of snow, the beloved Sleeping Giant, or 6,792-foot Beartooth Mountain as the maps label it, rules the northern skyline. Across the Missouri River Canyon from this sentinel, two of the most prominent peaks in the Gates of the Mountains Wilderness, 7,443-foot Candle Mountain and 7,980-foot Moore's Mountain are clearly visible. Then comes the unmistakable long Hog Back Ridge at 7,813 feet. Looking a bit farther south, 8,942-foot Boulder Baldy and 8,810-foot Boulder Mountain jut up above the surrounding forest. To the east near Townsend, the regal beauty of the two monarchs of the range, 9,467-foot Mount Baldy and 9,480-foot Mount Edith is reflected in the mirror of Canyon Ferry Lake.

Folks in White Sulphur Springs and the Smith River Valley who contemplate these mountains from their gentler sunrise side, declare some ownership as well.

▲ The Sleeping Giant, listed on maps as Beartooth Mountain, is an outlier of the Big Belts.
JOHN LAMBING

▲ The Twin Silos
and Canyon
Ferry Lake
– the Big Belt
Mountains in the
distance
RICK AND SUSIE GRAETZ

◄ Outsiders as
well as locals
enjoy fishing the
various waters
around Helena.
DONNY SEXTON/
TRAVEL MONTANA

Lewis and Clark duly noted the stretch of the Missouri River slicing through the Big Belts. Clark came first, camping on the night of July 18, 1805, a bit west of today's Ming Bar. The next day he continued up the Missouri and out into what is now the Helena or Prickly Pear Valley, just to the east of the interstate. On July 19, he stopped for the evening near present day Lakeside.

Lewis and his contingent, following behind, spent the night of the 18th, a short distance down-river from today's upper Holter Lake. On July 19, 1805, he noted in his journals, *"this evening we entered the most remarkable clifts that we have yet seen. these clifts rise from the waters edge on either side perpendicularly to the hight of 1200 feet. every object here wears a dark and gloomy aspect. the tow[er]ing and projecting rocks in many places seem ready to tumble on us. the river appears to have forced it's way through this immence body of solid rock for the distance of 5¾ Miles and where it makes it's exit below has th[r]own on either side vast collumns of rocks mountains high. the river appears to have woarn a passage just the width of it's channel or 150 yds. it is deep from side to side nor is there in the 1st 3 Miles of this distance a spot except one of a few yards in extent on which a man could rest the soal of his foot. it was late in the evening before I entered this place and was obliged to continue my rout untill sometime after dark before I found a place sufficiently large to encamp my small party ... from the singular appearance of this place I called it the gates of the rocky mountains."*

Somewhat flooded today by the backed up waters of Holter Lake, these Gates of the Mountains are just as magnificent as when the Corps of Discovery first beheld them.

Western Montana was founded on placer gold and the Big Belts lent a hand. While the better known Last Chance Gulch gave birth to Helena, in 1864, three former Confederate soldiers discovered gold in a steep narrow canyon heading east of today's Canyon Ferry Lake and christened the area Confederate Gulch.

Diamond City, its *"capital,"* was supposedly so named because the initial four cabins formed a diamond pattern in the snow-covered landscape. Sprouting almost overnight, by 1867, an estimated 10,000 people were living in the town and throughout the gulch. In 1870 though, the good times and the gold played out; virtually nothing remains today.

Natural features and recreation opportunities abound in the Big Belts. Dry and not as lofty as other Montana ranges, they do provide an excellent system of trails and great wildlife habitat. And since the snow leaves these mountains early, it's a popular destination for spring hiking.

On and below the northern slopes of the Belts, the 32,318-acre Beartooth Game Range offers a haven for almost every big game animal found in Montana. Osprey frequent its river border, a sizable elk herd roams freely and in 1805, Lewis and Clark's journals noted the abundance of bighorn sheep in the area. The reserve rolls out in what seems like gentle country, but the eastern boundary along Shellrock Ridge rises in an impressive bit of relief, almost 4,288 feet above its lowest point. Managed by the Montana Department of Fish Wildlife and Parks, the range is accessed from Holter Lake.

This wildlife sanctuary is contiguous to the very rugged 28,562-acre Gates of the Mountains Wilderness. Picturesque limestone escarpments that plunge precipitously and steep, forested mountainsides are hallmarks of Montana's smallest wilderness area. Fifty two miles of maintained trails amble throughout. Candle Mountain, an easy climb from the favorite backpacking destination of Bear Prairie, provides amazing views of the far reaching landscape.

▲ Mount Baldy is a sentinel of the Big Belt Mountains.
JOHN LAMBING

◀ From the road between Montana City and East Helena looking toward East Helena and the Big Belt Mountains.
RICK AND SUSIE GRAETZ

▶ Refrigerator
Canyon in the
Gates of the
Mountains
Wilderness
JOHN REDDY

A 16-mile footpath leads through Refrigerator Canyon and across to Meriwether Landing on the Missouri River. A day-trip for some hearty souls, most overnight in Bear Prairie. Through the warm months, a tour boat stops at the landing and will ferry campers to Upper Holter Lake for a fee. Hikers and horseback riders should be aware that water and horsefeed in this Wilderness is scarce.

The road to the Duck Creek Pass area, northeast of Townsend and above the east side of Canyon Ferry Lake, opens up a beautiful and different part of the range. From the pass, one trail heads north to the ridgeline between the summits of Boulder Mountain and Boulder Baldy, two miles apart. A path drops sharply from the ridge to the two Boulder lakes on the the north side. This easy to reach place is part of the 30,000-acre Camas Creek Roadless Area.

Walking south from Duck Creek Pass, it's possible to follow a high divide leading to the summit of Mt. Baldy and then four miles further to Mt. Edith where mountain goats frequent the tundra-like terrain. Other trails descend into Birch Creek Basin, the glacial cirque below the north face of the two peaks. A dozen lakes, reached via horseback and hiking paths, are scattered throughout this roadless enclave. Granite spires, called The Needles, tower above one of the lakes.

For those with a desire for motorized recreation, the Big Belts offer ample routes. Roads in two different directions from York, one via Trout Creek to Vigilante Campground and the other to Beaver Creek and the southern fringe of the Gates of the Mountains Wilderness, as well as Hogback Ridge, show the most spectacular scenery. The towering limestone walls and pinnacles are awesome. Numerous hiking trails emanate from the roads.

▲ Canyon Ferry Lake, popular for boating and swimming in the summer months, sits just below the southern slopes of the Big Belt Mountains.

DONNIE SEXTON/
TRAVEL MONTANA

58

▲ In the Big Belt
Mountains
looking toward
the Prickly Pear
Valley.
RICK AND SUSIE GRAETZ

▶ The Lewis and
Clark County
Fair brings
country-folk and
city-folk together
RICK AND SUSIE GRAETZ

Smooth and deep, the Missouri river flows from Upper Holter to Holter Lake on the north perimeter of the range and opens watercraft access to the Belts. A tour boat operates through the Gates of the Mountains from the marina on Upper Holter.

Major fires have also visited the Big Belt Mountains, including one of the most infamous infernos in Montana's history, the Mann Gulch Fire. Adjacent to the big wall Lewis dubbed *"gates of the rocky mountains"* and a short way downstream from Meriwether Campground, Mann Gulch ascends steeply from the Missouri River's east side. It was here on August 5, 1949, that a lightning ignited wildfire over-ran a crew of 16 smokejumpers, trapping them in the narrow gulch. Only three survived. Norman Maclean's book Young Men and Fire details the sad tragedy.

On November 13, 1990, during an unusual dry period for that time of the year, a discarded cigarette caused almost 80 percent of the Beartooth Game Range to burn. And in the summer of 2000, more than 29,000 acres in Cave Gulch and the Magpie Creek Road east of Canyon Ferry Lake went up in flames. At almost the same time, a large fire burning in the southern fringes of the range, in the vicinity of Deep Creek Canyon, scorched 10,000-plus acres of Forest Service Land on both sides of the road over Deep Creek Pass from Townsend to White Sulphur Springs.

The Big Belts and its wildlands' roads and trails are popular for all forms of recreation, especially in the Helena and Townsend areas. As a result, conflicts and problems arise. For the most part though, motorized use of the area seems to be compatible enough with those enjoying hiking, cross country skiing, horseback riding and other quiet activities. However, illegal off-road motor vehicle use has emerged as the number one problem for the US Forest Service and Bureau of Land Management, the agencies responsible for the Belts. As this unauthorized use is spreading, sportsmen and recreationists alike are concerned. With plenty of routes to use in these hills, there is no need to go off road with vehicles.

The Helena National Forest map has complete coverage of the Big Belts. It also lists the USGS topo maps needed for specific locations.

The precipitous forested slopes, high bare ridges, lake basins, nearly vertical jagged limestone escarpments and narrow steep gulches in the canyons of the Big Belts, are a treasure. Their easy access is inviting.

▸ The Gates of
the Mountains
were named
by Meriwether
Lewis in July
of 1805.
RICK AND SUSIE GRAETZ

The Gates of the Mountains Wilderness
by Rick and Susie Graetz

When you look toward the northern horizon from Helena, the foothills and mountains seem to blend together in a continuously forested belt, separating the Helena Valley from the prairie farther north.

The distant view is deceiving. Out in those hills, the massive Missouri River has carved its path through the limestone, leaving towering walls that Lewis and Clark called *"The Gates of the Mountains."* About 10 miles to the east of this formation, a scenic road along Beaver Creek also is bordered by spectacular cliffs. In between lies Helena's backyard wilderness, The Gates of the Mountains.

The high peaks that characterize Glacier National Park, the Madison Range, the Beartooth and other Montana wilderness areas are missing. In their place, picturesque limestone escarpments and gentle forested mountains reside. At 28,562 acres, it is one of Montana's smaller wilderness areas.

A wilderness experience in every way, the Gates offers an excellent trail system leading through high meadows, open forests and narrow gorges cut by streams. Elk, deer, bears, mountain lions, mountain goats, coyotes and golden eagles frequent the area. In the spring, wildflowers hold court. Summer brings a bright green moss-like phlox covering much of the limestone outcroppings as well as the lower parts of the cliffs.

The trails are simple to negotiate and no single trip through the country requires more than two days. For the strong hiker, a one-day, 16-mile walk crosses the area.

Human use here is low, and the opportunity for solitude is high. About 53 miles of well marked, maintained trails are ready for use.

However, water and horse feed are scarce. The Hunter's Gulch and Refrigerator Canyon trails have stock unloading ramps and hitching rails.

The most popular trip commences at Refrigerator Canyon, about 13 miles north of York, and comes out at Meriwether Landing, on the Missouri River, some 16 miles away. Refrigerator Canyon is a dramatic sight. A deep narrow gorge, just a little wider than a horse, escapes the sunlight and funnels the wind, resulting in a temperature many degrees colder than outside the canyon. The trail passes through the forest, winding its way up the mountainside, gaining elevation slowly.

The mid-way point is Bear Prairie. This high meadow offers water, good views, a place to camp and a chance to climb 7,443-foot Candle Mountain. From its summit, the Helena Valley, Rocky Mountain Front and Bob Marshall Wilderness are visible. Those who know their mountains will also be able to identify the Flint Creek and Mission ranges. From Bear Prairie the trail eventually drops sharply down through Meriwether Canyon to the Missouri, where tour boats stop several times a day. Hikers can finish the trip with a pleasant boat ride out.

A shuttle car and knowledge of the boat schedule are helpful.

For those not wishing to take the boat, another trail from Bear Prairie descends Big Log Gulch to Hunters Gulch and out to Nelson, about five miles from Refrigerator Canyon. Two cars would be useful here as well.

62

▲ Early season canoeing on Upper Holter Lake near the entrance to the Gates of the Mountains.
RICK AND SUSIE GRAETZ

▶ Bear Prairie is a preferred camping spot in the Gates of the Mountains Wilderness.
RICK AND SUSIE GRAETZ

The northern portions of the wilderness are reached from Wolf Creek via a road that runs along Holter Lake to the Beartooth Game Ranch. From here you can, with the aid of a compass and map, reach Mann Gulch and an overlook of the Missouri River. Mann Gulch is the sight of the disastrous 1948 forest fire that took the lives of 13 smokejumpers. Trail 260 is a route that runs along the northern perimeter of the wilderness, with a steep trail going south to Bear Prairie and a trail that winds up in the vicinity of 7,980-foot Moors Mountain — the highest peak in the Gates of the Mountain Wilderness.

Take a full day to hike up Spring Gulch to a divide, then head down Fields Gulch to the Missouri River. This area is in the southwestern part of the wilderness, and reached, via the American Bar Road, from Nelson on the Beaver Creek Road out of York. The Gates of the Mountains is void of lakes. Streams and springs throughout the area provide periodic water, but since this is dry country, bring plenty of your own. Willow, Moors, Porcupine and Hunters creeks are reliable for water. Small springs such as Bear Prairie and Turnout are also dependable.

The Gates of the Mountains offers perhaps the longest visiting season of any of Montana's wilderness areas. Owing to its lower elevation and the semi-arid climate of the surrounding area, the snow is often gone by mid May and trail blocking snows usually hold off until October. The flowers are at their best in June and July. Early autumn displays beautiful color in the lower elevations and up in the meadows. Seeing this place, can best be described as a very nice encounter; not something that will overwhelm you like the high alpine country.

The Forest Service map of The Gates of the Mountains Wilderness shows all the above mentioned trails and roads and points out places to get water. The Helena National Forest Supervisor's office and the Helena Ranger Station, both located in Helena, have the map.

◄ Susan Hansen in the Gates of the Mountains Wilderness looking out on the Big Belt Mountains.
RICK AND SUSIE GRAETZ

THE ELKHORN MOUNTAINS
by Rick and Susie Graetz with Jodie Canfield

Nearly 300,000 acres in bulk — 21 miles long and 19 miles wide — the Elkhorn Mountains are a part of the high rim of peaks circling the Prickly Pear Valley and Helena, Montana's capital town.

Along with their visual beauty, the Elkhorns are a vital ingredient in the quality of life to all who live near them.

Due to their location atop the Boulder batholith, complex best describes the geology of the Elkhorns. As a refresher in Geology 101, a batholith is an intrusion and extrusion of molten magma from deep within the earth. Here it intruded into the Elkhorn's sedimentary foundation as well as extruding over it. The original basement rocks shows through in places on the south side of the mountains. Then another earthly process happened to further complicate matters.

According to Dave Alt, University of Montana professor and author, enormous volumes of magma (molten rock) from underneath the Boulder batholith erupted to build the volcanic pile we call the Elkhorns. This magma spewed over the surface and crystallized into mostly andesite, an igneous rock. Andesite is a rock common to volcanoes and is formed when magma or lava (lava is magma that makes it to the earth's exterior) reaches the surface and cools.

It was this batholith and its proximity to the sedimentary rocks of limestone, which make up much of the Helena area, that led to the discovery of the gold that spawned Helena and surrounding gold camps (mineralization is usually found in the contact zone between the igneous and sedimentary rocks). Gold and silver were discovered in the Elkhorn Mountains in 1870 and led to the founding of the town of Elkhorn in the southern end of the mountains in 1883.

In the late 1880s, almost 700 people lived there. Silver was the predominant treasure and the vein that produced it played out in 1912, thus ending large-scale mining there. Today the place is an home to only a few residents.

Missing from the Elkhorns are the jagged and rocky peaks found to the north in Glacier National Park and along the Rocky Mountain Front. Most of the summits of the Elkhorns are timbered and the few that do reach above timberline have a relatively rounded profile. Glacier carved cirques flank the north faces of two of the highest summits — 9,414-foot Crow Peak and 9,381-foot Elkhorn Peak.

Below these uplifts, Tizer Basin cradles lakes and open parklands. Other components of the landscape include meadows, creeks, waterfalls and wildlife. Accessed by a substantial road and trail network, this island mountain range has all the attributes needed for a casual drive or a week-long backcountry experience.

A forested ridgeline, as seen from the Prickly Pear Valley, shows the scar of the 47,000-acre Warm Springs Fire, caused by sparks from a vehicle in 1988.

The Elkhorn's claim to fame is its wildlife. In simple terms, the *"Horns"* are considered to be the most productive elk habitat in Montana. Here, 160,000 acres of forestlands represent the only Wildlife Management Unit in the National Forest system.

A joint publication produced by the Montana Fish, Wildlife and Parks, the U.S. Forest Service and the Bureau of Land Management explains the situation well. In 1974, Senator Lee Metcalf intro-

▲ South of Helena, a field awaits spring planting – the Elkhorn Mountains in the distance. RICK AND SUSIE GRAETZ

◀ Looking toward the Montana City area and the Elkhorn Mountains from the road between Montana City and East Helena. RICK AND SUSIE GRAETZ

▶ The Gurnett family
hiking in the Elkhorn
Mountains below
Strawberry Butte.
RICK AND SUSIE GRAETZ

▲ The historic
Kleffner Ranch
at East Helena.
RICK AND SUSIE GRAET

▶ A tough day
fishing on
Gipsy Lake in
the Elkhorn
Mountains.
JODIE CANFIELD

duced a statewide wilderness study act containing 10 National Forest roadless areas, which included a portion of the Elkhorn Mountains.

But by the mid-1970s, the Helena National Forest issued a plan that called for compromising the roadless portion of the Elkhorns by constructing roads and harvesting timber. Thirteen conservation groups filed an administrative appeal against implementation of the plan.

On Labor Day in 1976, Senator John Melcher held a hearing in Helena to consider the pros and cons of creating a designated wilderness area in the Elkhorns. Following the hearing, Melcher separated the Elkhorns out of the statewide study act and introduced legislation establishing a separate study for the Elkhorns. Congress directed the Helena and Deerlodge national forests to evaluate about 86,000 acres of these mountains for possible inclusion in the wilderness preservation system.

Comments on the wilderness study were wide-ranging, but almost everyone wanted wildlife protected even if they were against the designated wilderness classification. At that point, Ruppert Cutler, assistant secretary of Agriculture, became interested in the Elkhorn controversy and envisioned a creative management approach outside of the Wilderness Act. The formal Record of Decision issued in 1981 recommended no wilderness designation, but that all 160,000 acres of Forest Service lands (to include more of the total ecosystems and key winter range areas that were outside of the Wilderness Study Areas) be recognized as a Wildlife Management Unit.

As part of the forest plan direction for the Elkhorns, a partnership with the Montana Department of Fish, Wildlife and Parks (FWP) was established to provide cooperation in the management and monitoring of wildlife in the Elkhorns. Then in 1992, the Helena and Deerlodge National Forests, the BLM, and Montana FWP signed a Memorandum of Understanding (MOU), which was an agreement to work together to *"manage the Elkhorns as a mountain range."*

The MOU established the Elkhorn Cooperative Management Area as a unique, cooperatively administered geographic area, where management of all lands within public ownership emphasizes sustainable ecosystems.

In addition, on non-Forest Service lands, where opportunities and authority allow, wildlife and recreation values are emphasized in concert with the direction for the Wildlife Management Unit on National Forest system lands.

The alliance to manage the Elkhorn's wildlife was strengthened in 1990 when the U.S. Forest Service hired Jodie Canfield — a wildlife biologist with experience working with all three of the management agencies in the Elkhorns — to serve as a coordinator and liaison officer among the agencies involved with the Wildlife Management Unit. This ensures that bureaucratic boundary lines are ignored in favor of a cooperative effort to protect both the wildlife and the wild character of the range. Canfield is optimistic that the Elkhorns will continue to provide an excellent model of interagency cooperation, but she cautions that the challenges are plentiful.

Incidentally, Canfield received the Rocky Mountain Elk Foundation's 2003 Elk Country Award for her outstanding work in the Elkhorns.

With the agencies functioning together and with partners that include the Rocky Mountain Elk Foundation and a citizens working group, the Elkhorns have been transformed.

As a result then, about 1,600 elk roam one of the largest elk winter ranges on public lands in the nation. In addition, MFWP started an innovative hunting season regulation in 1987 that allows for the legal harvest of spike bulls with a general license, and the permit-only taking of branch-antlered bulls. The result is unique — a hunted population with lots of bull elk of all ages, including some 14-15 years olds sporting giant racks. It is no wonder hunting and elk viewing is so popular in Helena's southwest mountain range.

Recently, the agencies transplanted bighorn sheep. Today the herd of approximately 120 sheep, inhabiting the eastern flank of the Elkhorns, is doing well and allows for some limited hunting opportunities. Mountain Goats, not native to the area, also were introduced in 1956 and hunted for many years. Today, with a declining population estimated at about 50 goats, hunting has been discontinued

Native westslope cutthroat trout are expanding in some of the streams due to an innovative restoration project.

Cattle still summer here, but grazing must meet a strict set of standards. Historically, fires helped shape the Elkhorns ecosystem, and both prescribed and wild fire now play a role in keeping grasslands healthy forests recycled. In some places, tree thinning has been used as a tool to create conditions where fire can be introduced without killing the forest.

In addition to the elk, the forests and meadows of the Elkhorns also support healthy populations of many other wildlife species including moose, mule deer and black bears. Astute observers occasionally see more elusive species, such as lynx and wolverine.

The legacy of the mining era left its scars and several abandoned mines have been cleaned up to support new grass and clear water. Just in time for the 200th birthday of the preservation of the Elkhorns as a forest reserve, the crown jewel of the Elkhorns, Crow Creek Falls, has been cleared of its mining refuse and returned to the public.

Access to the Elkhorns is plentiful and roads lead to the roadless country from almost all directions. Recreationists can experience the Elkhorns from two different historic cabins that can be rented, from the many creek-side camping sites, on a Sunday drive to the historic town of Elkhorn from Boulder, and on the many trails leading to the more remote portions of the mountain range. A waterproof map is now available that shows all the roads and trails and camping areas in the Elkhorn Mountain Range.

Some of the roads trace old wagon routes once used by prospectors and Indians and trappers at one time traversed a few of the interior trails. It's this roadless center of approximately 54,000 acres that makes the range an attractive place for both wildlife and recreationists. The Elkhorn Travel Plan was completed in 1995 and provides a balanced set of opportunities for both motorized and non-motorized interests. Both the Forest Plan and the Travel Plan prohibit motorized uses in the core area in order to provide seclusion and security for wildlife and solitude for those who seek it.

▲ Looking north down Canyon Ferry Lake from the Missouri River's inlet.
LARRY MAYER

◀ Helena's beautiful mountains and blue-sky days make a perfect backdrop for outdoor weddings. Dave Tudor walks his daughter Olivia down the aisle.
RICK AND SUSIE GRAETZ

▲ The Helena
   Arsenal Soccer
   Champs in August
   1991. Soccer is fast
   becoming the most
   popular sport
   in Helena.
   RICK AND SUSIE GRAETZ

▶ Dressed for the
   4th of July.
   RICK AND SUSIE GRAETZ

THE CORP OF DISCOVERY IN LEWIS AND CLARK AND BROADWATER COUNTIES
by Rick and Susie Graetz

On July 15, 1805, after having completed the portage of the *"great falls"* and making the canoes they needed, the Corps of Discovery left their camp east of Ulm. The next segment of their journey took them through a transition zone from the prairie across big valleys into the mountains themselves. Much of their route from here to the Three forks can be seen from Interstate 15 and side roads which parallel their path on water and land for most of the way. Where the course veers from the roadway, it's possible to boat up and down the Missouri and the lakes it now forms. When the trail enters the Prickly Pear Valley, roads once more approximate a good deal of the distance south.

By the 18th of July, the captains had split up, Clark traveled on land and Lewis stayed with the canoes. According to Lewis and Clark scholar and mapmaker Robert Bergantino, *"Clark probably left the Missouri River near Holter Dam and continued south-southeast to Falls Gulch. He then followed that gulch to Towhead Gulch and down that to Hilger Valley. Clark's camp appears to be south of the summit of the pass on Towhead Gulch about two miles west of Beartooth Mountain (The Sleeping Giant)."*

⏶ North of Helena, a fly-fisherman's drift boat eases down the Missouri.

RICK AND SUSIE GRAETZ

74

Lewis now was maneuvering up the Missouri through a winding, mixed terrain of canyons and narrow valleys. His camp on the 18th was somewhere in the vicinity of the center of Lower Holter Lake.

On July 19th, Lewis's contingent was passing through today's Gates of the Mountains Recreation Area, which extends between Lower Holter and Holter lakes. In Lewis's words, *"The Musquetoes are very troublesome to us as usual ... whever we get a view of the lofty summits of the mountains the snow presents itself, altho we are almost suffocated in this confined vally with heat ... this evening we entered much the most remarkable clifts that we have yet seen. these clifts rise from the waters edge on either side perpendicularly to the hight of about 1200 feet. every object here wears a dark and gloomy aspect. the towering and projecting rocks in many places seem ready to tumble on us ... for the distance of 5 3/4 miles ... the river appears to have woarn a passage just the width of it's channel or 150 yds. it is deep from side to side nor is ther in the 1st 3 miles of this distance a spot... on which a man could rest the soal of his foot...it happens fortunately that altho the current is strong it is not so much so but what it may be overcome with the oars for there is hear no possibility of using either the cord or Setting pole. it was late in the evening before I entered this place and was obliged to continue my rout untill sometime after dark before I found a place sufficiently large to encamp my small party ... from the singular appearance of this place I called it the gates of the rocky mountains."* During the summer, there is an interpretive tour by boat from Holter Lake through the Gates.

▲ Helena's downtown area, looking north to the Big Belt Mountains.
RICK AND SUSIE GRAETZ

▲ The sweet
springtime scent
of apple blossoms
fills a Helena
neighborhood.
RICK AND SUSIE GRAETZ

◀ The Vigilante
Parade is a
tradition with
Helena's high
school crowd.
RICK AND SUSIE GRAETZ

The Governor's Cup Race, held the first week in June, attracts thousands of runners to the city.
JON EBELT

Clark was following an old Indian road, which took him from the Sieben Flats area past the Hilger Ranch to the south end of Holter Lake, there he crossed the hilly lands to the east of today's North Pass at Interstate 15 and traversed the east side of Lake Helena where he *"passed a hansome valley watered by a large creek* (Ordway Creek to them and now Prickly Pear Creek, which connects Lake Helena to Hauser Lake)," and rested for the night near Lakeside on Hauser Lake.

Leaving the impressive Gates of the Mountains on the 20th, Lewis describes, *"the hills retreated from the river and the valley became wider than we have seen since we entered the mountains."* Noticing a column of smoke coming from a nearby valley, *"we were at a loss to determine whether it had been set on fire by the natives as a signal among themselves on discovering us ... or whether it had been set on fire by Capt. C. and party accedentally. the first however proved to be the fact ... in the evening ... we encamped on the Lard. side near a spring on a high bank the prickly pears are so abundant that we could scarcely find room to lye. just above our camp the river is again closed in by the Mouts. on both sides."* They were about one half mile below the bridge crossing Hauser Lake on Route 280 to York.

In departing this camp, Lewis wrote, *"Capt. Clark set out early and proceeded on through a valley leaving the river about six miles to his left; he fell in with an old Indian road which he pursued untill it struck the river about 18 miles from his camp of the last evening just above the entrance of a large creek which we call white paint Creek.* (probably Beaver Creek, mid-way down the west side of Canyon Ferry Lake) ... *the party were so much fortiegued with their march and their feet cut with*

The Great Northern Town Center.

RICK AND SUSIE GRAETZ

the flint and perced with the prickly pears untill they had become so painfull that he proceeded but liitle further before he determined to encamp on the river and wait my arrival."

Lewis's water route, snaking through alternating narrow canyons of the Missouri to open meadows, passed American Bar along Holter Lake and White Sandy and Black Sandy beaches and the entrance to Prickly Pear Creek, all on Hauser Lake. Clark came in direct touch with today's Prickly Pear Valley, the first of the big intermountain valleys they would encounter. From here they would travel through the area now covered by Canyon Ferry Lake, a wide valley that stretches from the Big Belt Mountains to the Elkhorns.

The July 21, 1805 journal notes for Lewis include, *"this morning we passed a bold creek ... this we called Pryor's Creek (Spokane Creek) after Sergt. Pryor one of our party."* The camp was about five miles above Canyon Ferry Dam and on the east side of the Spokane Hills. It would have been close to where Avalanche Creek enters the Missouri on its west side.

Still on Canyon Ferry Lake, Lewis meets up with the sore-footed Clark. The united group paddles its way upstream a few miles above Beaver Creek, camping on the left side of the river. The campsites of the past two days are now under the waters of the lake.

Clark was determined to continue on foot in search of the Shoshone. Though nearly crippled, he followed an Indian road (still faintly visible) and spent the evening of July 23 about four miles below Toston. That same day, Lewis met Duck Creek where it entered the Missouri and named it *"Whitehous's Creek after Josph. Whitehouse one of the party."* His camp that night was at the upper end of Canyon

▲ Boating on Hauser Lake.

▲ The Fighting
Saints, Carroll
College's
football team,
won the small
college national
championship in
2002 and 2003.
JON EBELT

◄ The notable
Blue Stone
building – now
a law firm
– and the historic
Guardian of the
Gulch fire tower.
RICK AND SUSIE GRAETZ

▲ Hayfields south
of Helena, the
Elkhorns in the
distance.
RICK AND SUSIE GRAETZ

▶ A Prickly Pear
Valley barn
receives a touch
of snow.
JOHN LAMBING

Ferry Lake probably in the area of the man-made bird nesting islands north of Townsend.

Early in the morning of the 24th, Lewis and his men *"passed a remarkable bluff of a crimson coloured earth on Stard. intermixed with Stratas of black and brick red slate."* From above these Crimson Bluffs, one can look up the main street of Townsend. Lewis spent that night about six miles farther upstream in the area of Dry Creek.

It was in this area, from atop a high hill Clark viewed a series of islands, which he drew on his map. Today, this fishing access site is now York's Islands in honor of Captain Clark's servant.

Traveling across the Crow Creek Valley, Clark camped that night about 16 air miles south of Lewis, in the broken hills and ridges along the Missouri, below Trident just short of the three forks.

Heading toward and then past Toston on the 25th, Lewis relates, *"the face of the country ... were the same as yesterday's, untill late in the evening, when the valley appeared to termineate and the river was again hemned in on both sides with high caiggy and rocky clifts* (to Clark this area between Lombard and Toston was *"Little Gate of the Mountain")* soon after entering these hills or lower mountains we passed a number of fine bold springs ... we passed a large Crk. today in the plain country ... we called Gass's Creek* (Crow Creek coming from the Elkhorn Mountains).

Finally on July 25, 1805, Captain Clark proclaims, *"a fine morning we proceeded on a few miles to the three forks of the Missouri."* On the morning of July 27th, Lewis and his men met up with Clark at the three forks.

▲ The former Federal Building, now houses the town of Helena's and Lewis and Clark County's offices.

RICK AND SUSIE GRAETZ

▶ Helena
homeowners are
avid gardeners.
RICK AND SUSIE GRAETZ

83

▲ The Oxbow
Bend on the
Missouri River
below the
Sleeping Giant.
LARRY MAYER

◄ The Western
Rendezvous
of Art at the
Montana
Historical
Society building
is just one
of the many
artistic venues
held in Helena.
DONNIE SEXTON/
TRAVEL MONTANA

▲ Iceboat sailing,
fishing and
skating make
good use of
Canyon Ferry
Lake in the winter.
RICK AND SUSIE GRAETZ

▶ The Bullwhacker
statue on the
walking mall.
JOHN LAMBING

◄ From near the
Spokane Hills,
looking toward
the northeast
and the Big Belt
Mountains.
RICK AND SUSIE GRAETZ

◄ The last sunrays
of the day cast
a rich light on
rocks of Mount
Helena and the
town below.
RICK AND SUSIE GRAETZ

▲ A reminder from
the past, the
yellow trolley on
the downtown
walking mall.
RICK AND SUSIE GRAETZ

▶ Snowboarders at
the Great Divide
Ski Area.

DONNIE SEXTON/
TRAVEL MONTANA

◄ Canyon Ferry

Lake.

DONNIE SEXTON/
TRAVEL MONTANA

▸ From near
the summit of
Mount Helena
looking out
toward Nevada
Mountain and
the Continental
Divide.
RICK AND SUSIE GRAETZ